Adventures in Wild Places

Written by Marilyn Woolley

Series Consultant: Linda Hoyt

WorldWise®
Content-based Learning

Contents

Chapter 1
Wild places

Imagine climbing to the top of the highest mountain, or diving into dark underwater caves. Imagine walking across frozen land marked by dangerous **crevasses** in a screaming **blizzard**, or **trekking** across hot deserts where water and shade are scarce. These are wild places where no one lives because the environment is harsh and it is difficult to survive. But some people like to go to these wild places for an adventure. These adventurers want to test themselves against the elements and hazards in ways that other people find hard to understand.

The weather in wild places can be severe and the conditions very dangerous. People who seek adventures in these harsh environments often have to travel great distances and spend a lot of money on equipment. They also undergo strict training and fitness programs. They do this to give themselves the best chance of surviving, in case they become sick or suffer life-threatening injuries. Wild places are often remote and medical help is far away.

This book examines the dangers of some wild places, and looks at what these adventurers do to stay safe and the equipment and technology they use.

Chapter 2
Underwater adventures

Many people like to explore the underwater world. For thousands of years, people have dived into the sea, not only to look at the wildlife wonders in the sea, but also to hunt fish and other sea animals for food. The greatest obstacle divers have to overcome is not being able to breathe under water.

Before air tanks were first used in 1943, people could only free-dive. This means that they held their breath under water. Free divers don't usually go very deep, because they need to come up often for air. The invention of air tanks, or scuba (self-contained underwater breathing apparatus) equipment, meant that divers could breathe under water. Not only could they dive deeper, they could also stay under water for a longer time.

?

Did you know?

The weight of the water pressing down on the ocean floor is called water pressure. On the ocean floor the water pressure can be 100 times greater than at the surface of the ocean. Some animals can survive here, but this part of the ocean is dangerous for humans.

Diving equipment

Divers use scuba equipment to explore the ocean.

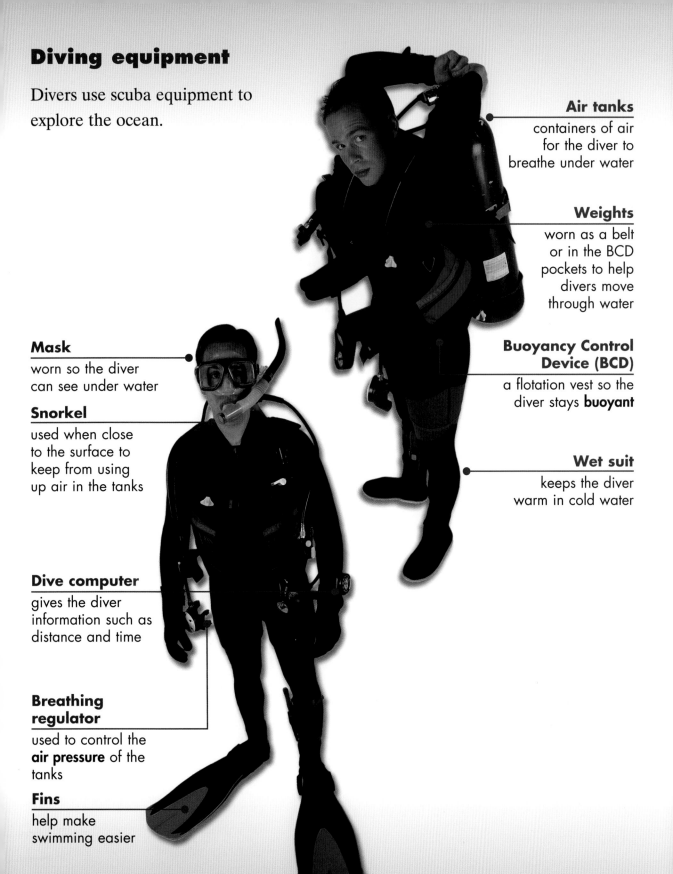

Air tanks
containers of air for the diver to breathe under water

Weights
worn as a belt or in the BCD pockets to help divers move through water

Buoyancy Control Device (BCD)
a flotation vest so the diver stays **buoyant**

Wet suit
keeps the diver warm in cold water

Mask
worn so the diver can see under water

Snorkel
used when close to the surface to keep from using up air in the tanks

Dive computer
gives the diver information such as distance and time

Breathing regulator
used to control the **air pressure** of the tanks

Fins
help make swimming easier

Hazards of diving

Even with scuba equipment, people have to be careful when diving. There may be problems with the gas supply (air) from the scuba equipment, and divers need to stay alert so that they don't get lost under water. But the main danger for divers is a condition known as the bends, or decompression sickness, which can be fatal.

People who dive undergo extensive training before diving. They must obtain a licence, which qualifies them to dive to different depths. The common diving depth for beginners is around 18 metres, while advanced divers can descend to a depth of up to 30 metres.

Here are some other diving tips for staying safe:

- always dive in pairs
- check that all equipment is working properly
- have a plan and stick to it
- maintain a good level of physical fitness
- practise removing your mask or weights under water during a safety stop.

What are the bends?

If divers rise to the surface too quickly, they can get the bends. The body finds it hard to cope with the sudden change in water pressure, and not enough **oxygen** gets into the blood. A diver can become partly **paralysed**, with severe pain in the chest and joints, cramps and breathing problems, and may drown.

Divers need a lot of training and practice to learn how to dive properly, use the equipment, and cope with the cold and pressure. They can avoid the bends by stopping at intervals while rising to the surface and focusing on breathing normally.

Decompression treatment can be used to help divers recover if they do get the bends. This is given in a small room, called a chamber, where the air pressure is slowly increased to reduce the feelings of sickness.

Did you know?

To avoid the bends, divers should rise to the surface more slowly than the slowest bubble they produce.

The entrance and interior of a decompression chamber

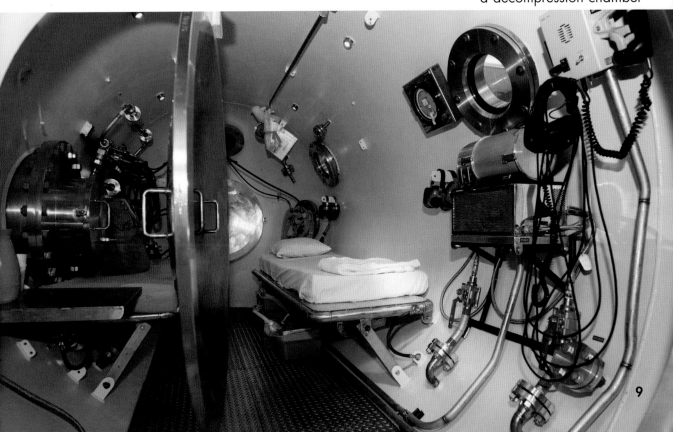

The challenge of ice diving

Ice divers dive under ice on lakes and at sea, and also under icebergs. Many people ice dive to see the beauty of sunlight on the ice overhead, while others do it to see marine life unique to a frozen climate. All ice divers are attracted by the challenge involved.

To stay safe, ice divers work in teams. The team cuts a hole in the ice and then two people dive into the water under the ice. They are attached to a rope that is held by two people on the surface. Two extra divers are also on the surface to help if something goes wrong. All ice divers carry a knife in case their rope is lost or cut. They can stab the knife into the ice so they are not dragged away by water currents and hold on until they are rescued.

Even with such safety measures, ice diving is more dangerous than sea diving because of the freezing cold temperatures that are harder on the human body. Ice divers also need to be careful not to get crushed by a moving iceberg or trapped under the ice. It can take days for rescue teams to arrive, because these wilder, frozen places are usually far away. Divers also need to be aware of animals such as polar bears that may attack.

Rope signals for ice divers

Divers under the ice and on the surface need to be able to communicate with each other. They do this by tugging on the safety rope. These signals can vary from one country to another, so it's important that the whole team uses the same signals. Here are the signals from a team that dives in the Arctic wilds.

Tugs	From	Means
1	Diver	Give me more line
1	Surface person	It's the end of the line
2	Diver	Okay
3	Diver	I'm returning, pull me up
3	Surface person	Stop the dive
3+	Diver	Something is wrong, pull me up

Chapter 3

Caving

A cave is a hole in a rock face that is sometimes large enough for people to enter. A cave system can have more than one entrance and may have many tunnels and **chambers**. Some caves can fill up with water.

Cavers are people who enjoy exploring caves. Not only do cavers walk long distances when exploring a cave system, but they also often have to climb down dark holes and crawl through narrow, slippery tunnels. Often these caves are in remote areas.

Mammoth Cave National Park in the United States is the longest cave system in the world, with more than 540 kilometres of tunnels.

Hazards of caving

Caves can be dangerous places. They can be wet and cold, and cavers can suffer from **hypothermia** if their body temperature drops severely. Because caves are dark, people can slip over, or fall down holes. Falling rocks can also hurt them.

In some caves, "foul air", sometimes called "bad air", can make people sick because not enough **oxygen** can get into the cave. It can cause headaches, dizziness and **fatigue**.

Another hazard of caving is cave fever. As cavers move about, soil is stirred up and breathed in. Some cave soil can carry a **fungus** that causes cave fever. This starts as a lung disease but may spread to other parts of the body and can end in death.

Stay safe while caving

- Wear protective clothing and shoes, which may include knee and elbow pads.
- Always go exploring in pairs or teams, so there is someone to help in case a caver is injured.
- Leave an **itinerary** with someone, so that if you get lost, you can be rescued.

Types of caves

Ice cave A cave that contains significant amounts of ice at all times and remains at temperatures below 0°C year round

Limestone cave
A cave where the old remains of sea animals have hardened into rock

Sea cave
A cave in the sea cliffs, formed by waves crashing against the rock over a long time

Wet cave
A cave that has a lake or stream deep enough to swim or wade through

13

Water-filled caves and their dangers

Divers use scuba equipment to explore caves filled with water. These caves sometimes have rare plants and animals. Cave diving has all the hazards of deep-sea diving, as well as the hazards of caving. Strong water currents can pull the diver in another direction, and parts of the cave walls may crumble easily. Divers can find it very hard to see, if sand becomes stirred up in the water.

Caves have ceilings and so divers must swim back to the entrance before rising to the water's surface. This can make things difficult if a cave diver needs to surface quickly in an emergency.

How cave divers keep safe

Like most adventure sports, cave divers operate in pairs or groups in case something goes wrong. They have a dive plan that includes how deep they will dive, how long the dive will last and any emergency procedures they may need to apply. Divers attach a long rope near the cave entrance, which is then carried on the dive through the cave. This way the group can keep track of where they've been and no one gets lost. To see in the dark, divers wear a helmet with a light attached to it, and carry spare batteries and bulbs.

Terrell

I love diving in caves as it is like being in another world. Every cave is full of water and totally dark. All you can see is the small area lit up by your torch.

It is a real adventure floating through the different caves, seeing new things all the time. I love the dark, shadowy shapes that form along the cave walls. They look like strange **moonscapes**.

A cave-diving experience

Terrell and Jana have been cave diving on the Yucatán Peninsula in Mexico. They each have their own point of view about diving in caves.

Jana

When you dive in caves, you are not only under ground, you are also completely under water. Everything is close to you, and you have to move very slowly so you don't disturb the dirt. It is totally silent, except for the sound of your own breathing through the scuba tanks.

I tried caving a few times with Terrell but I did not like feeling so closed in. I prefer sunny open spaces, like the beach.

Chapter 4

Adventures in the desert

Deserts are tough environments to survive in. They can be hot and dry, far away from the sea, or freezing cold places like Antarctica. Long ago, explorers would cross vast deserts to discover new lands. Those who go on desert **treks** today are inspired to test themselves against the environment, and are drawn to these remote, wild places.

Hazards of hot deserts

In hot deserts, the dry heat can make things unbearable. Travellers need to protect themselves from sunburn. They also need to watch out for deadly desert spiders and scorpions. As well, sudden sandstorms and dust storms can cause people to get lost.

Perhaps the biggest danger of all is the lack of drinking water, which can lead to **dehydration** and possible death. Desert travellers should be careful of drinking water they come across in case it is unclean and makes them sick.

Arita Baaijens

Did you know?

Another solo desert trekker is Robyn Davidson, who, in 1977, set out with four camels and a dog to trek 2,735 kilometres across the deserts of Central and Western Australia. Many years later, she undertook a similar journey across northwest India. Find out more about Robyn's treks and how she survived.

A solo desert trek

Africa is made up of many hot, wild deserts. Dutch woman Arita Baaijens first began riding camels in some of these deserts 20 years ago. Her first solo **expedition** was a 200-kilometre hike with three camels across the Western Desert of Egypt. In 2000, Baaijens organized a six-week, 1,600-kilometre solo trek in Sudan. Since then Baaijens has set off each year on a month-long desert journey, photographing and writing about her trip. She spends up to seven hours a day riding a camel and sleeps out under the stars each night.

A dangerous crevasse

Dangers of cold deserts

Cold polar deserts have their own dangers. As well as avoiding dehydration, adventurers have to be careful not to drink **stagnant water**. This contains bacteria that can cause fever and illness. There is also the danger of suffering **hypothermia** and **frostbite**.

Injuries can result from falling on ice or into **crevasses**. Poor visibility caused by thick fog, snowstorms or **blizzards** can cause adventurers to become lost.

Polar desert adventurer

Sir Douglas Mawson is a renowned explorer of the Antarctic wilds. He joined a team led by explorer Ernest Shackleton to go to Antarctica in August 1907. Once there, they experienced weather conditions that made everyday tasks, such as gathering fresh snow for drinking and cooking, a major achievement. A group of six men from this team, including Mawson, were the first to climb to the top of Mount Erebus, Antarctica's active volcano.

The expedition team trekked across the ice in one of the coldest and windiest places on Earth, where temperatures can drop as low as –85 degrees Celsius, with winds of up to 160 kilometres an hour during storms. Some men fell in crevasses and had to be rescued, while others suffered severe frostbite and **dysentery**. Fortunately, all members of this expedition survived, and they left Antarctica in February 1909.

Route of Australasian Antarctic Expedition, 1911

On the map:
Australia
Adelaide
Hobart
Macquarie Island
Antarctic Circle
pack ice pack ice pack ice
base camp
Antarctica
Mt Erebus

An epic sledge journey

In 1911, Mawson led the first Australasian Antarctic Expedition. He and his group sailed in the ship *Aurora* through more than 1,500 kilometres of pack ice to chart the Antarctic coastline. During a journey out from base camp, one member of his team fell into a snow-covered crevasse and died, along with a pack of dogs carrying their food supplies.

On the long return trek back to base, Mawson and his surviving partner, Mertz, had to eventually eat the remaining dogs. Mertz then got food poisoning, which led to his death. Now travelling solo, Mawson took another month to reach the base camp. He endured further blizzards along the way and twice fell down a crevasse. He later wrote about his near-death experiences in the book, *The Home of the Blizzard*.

19

Chapter 5

Rock climbing

Rock climbers love the challenge of climbing a sheer rock face in the wilds. What looks impossible to many people poses an exciting challenge to rock climbers. Rocks and cliffs are ranked on their steepness and how difficult they are to climb.

Stay safe while climbing

To climb well and safely, people need to be fit, have the right equipment and know enough about the cliffs they're climbing.

All climbers need to:
• check the weather before starting
• know what to do if storms, lightning strikes or bushfires occur
• carry extra clothing in case they get cold or wet
• avoid climbing on wet rock as it is slippery and less sturdy

Climbers mainly work in pairs. One person will start to climb while the other remains standing, though the climbers stay connected by ropes. These ropes are used to help with the climb. If it is a steep rock face, the two climbers may swap the lead many times, taking turns to control the rope for each other.

Word signals used by climbers

There can be a fair distance between two climbers on a rock face, so they need short terms that are understandable when shouted out. Here are some terms they use:

On belay?

A question from a climber to make sure their partner is ready to anchor and protect them.

Off belay!

A word signal given when a climber has reached a safe place and no longer requires protection from their partner.

Up rope!

A signal shouted by a climber when a tighter belay is needed.

belay
device

carabiners

Rock climbing equipment

helmet – worn to protect the head in case of a fall or loose rocks falling from above

harness – a strong **nylon** belt with leg loops that secures the climber to the rope

ropes – used for climbing up the mountain and connecting the climbers in a **belaying** team

carabiners – metal clips used to join the ropes together

belay device – a mechanism that helps to control the rope as a person climbs

climbing footwear – has a soft rubber sole for better grip on the rock face

What is cystic fibrosis?

Cystic fibrosis is a disease that some people are born with. It causes mucus to build up in organs in the body, especially the lungs and pancreas. It can make breathing very difficult, and can cause infections that damage the lungs.

Interview with a rock climber

Rock climbing can be dangerous and requires effort, but some people overcome a disability or major illness to do this sport. In this interview, Tom, who suffers from cystic fibrosis, talks about his rock climbing adventures and gives some safety tips.

Q: How did you get interested in rock climbing?

A: I'd never thought about rock climbing until I went camping in the wilds with my cousin and his friend. We did a couple of short, easy climbs. I thought I'd never make it, but when I reached the top, I was hooked.

Q: How did you learn more about climbing?

A: I began practising regularly. As a beginner, I trained with more experienced climbers so I could learn how to use the climbing equipment properly.

Q: What things do you do to keep fit?

A: It might sound silly, but really the best training for climbing is climbing. I go to an indoor climbing centre to keep fit when I can't get to a real rock.

Q: What have you learned about recognising danger?

A: I have learned to see the warning signs. Now, I am more likely to take safety measures to prevent a bad accident.

Popular rock-climbing sites

Mount Arapiles in Victoria is one of Australia's most popular rock-climbing places. It has more than 2,000 climbing routes.

The walls of deep gorges in the Blue Mountains in New South Wales are popular for climbing. One famous series of rocks in the area, Three Sisters, is now closed to climbers because of overuse.

Mount Arapiles, Victoria

Q: What are some of your goals for climbing?

A: I am always trying to push myself to do climbs that are more difficult. The difficulty of the climb can depend on how good the hand and footholds on the rocks are and how far apart these are, how steep the rock is and how long the climb is. The first person to do a climb ranks it and other climbers then confirm this rank.

Q: What else can you tell people about this sport?

A: Whether you are a beginner or an expert, the challenge is to achieve something you never thought you could do. The reward is the physical nature of climbing, along with the beauty of the natural world, making it unlike any other sport.

Tom's tips for belaying with a partner

1. Always choose someone you can trust as a partner.
2. Check each other's equipment and ropes.
3. Practise the word signals that you both will use for safety.
4. Communicate with each other all the time.
5. If you get into a tricky situation, keep calm by taking steady breaths.
6. Take short backward leaps when descending so that you remain in control.

Chapter 6

Adventures on mountains

Some people feel a real excitement when they climb mountains. They love being away from their normal environment and testing their fitness on rugged mountain ranges.

The environment at the top of mountains can be very harsh. The weather conditions are extreme, often with below-freezing temperatures, snowstorms and gale-force winds. People cannot live permanently in such wild environments and most people consider these places too dangerous and difficult to go near.

Did you know?

Mount Everest was named in 1865 after the British surveyor, Sir George Everest, who was the first person to record its height and location. In Nepal, they call the mountain Sagarmatha, while the Tibetan people know it as Chomolungma.

Mount Everest high achievers

The goal of a mountaineer is to climb the highest mountains. The biggest physical challenge is Mount Everest, the highest land mountain in the world. More than 1,500 people worldwide have climbed Mount Everest. Here are some of the notable ones:

1953: Sir Edmund Hillary from New Zealand and **Sherpa** Tenzing Norgay from Nepal are the first people to climb to the **summit**.

1963: James Whittaker is the first American to reach the top.

1975: Junko Tabei from Japan is the first woman to climb to the top of the mountain. She has since climbed the highest mountain on each continent.

2010: Jordan Romero from the United States, at age 13, is the youngest person to climb to the top.

2013: Yuichiro Miura from Japan, at age 80, is the oldest person to climb to the top.

Hazards on mountains

High mountains may have steep, slippery sides, and their tops can be covered in snow. Strong winds, rain, shifting snow and ice, rivers and streams can cause rocks to suddenly move or fall.

On snow-covered mountains, climbers can fall into **crevasses** or slip on ice. They can be hurt or even killed by avalanches, when large chunks of ice and snow rush downhill without warning. On very high mountains, there is not much **oxygen** in the air, which means climbers can find it difficult to breathe.

Mount Everest fact file

Located: in the Himalayan ranges on the border between Nepal and Tibet, China

Height: 8,848 metres

Average summit temperature:

Winter (December–February): –36° Celsius

Summer (July–September): –19° Celsius

Wind speeds: more than 285 kilometres per hour (in winter)

Health risks

As climbing sports become more popular, some doctors are very alarmed about the health risks of high **altitude**. The higher people climb, the more their bodies have to adjust to the lack of oxygen in the air and the extremely low temperatures. The following table shows the types of illnesses climbers can suffer, setting out their causes and **symptoms**, and how they can be treated, or, better still, prevented.

	Altitude sickness	Hypothermia
Illnesses and causes	Occurs when climbers don't get enough oxygen to breathe the higher they climb. It can cause problems including brain and breathing functions, sharp chest pains and respiratory failure. Can happen at 2,400 metres above sea level.	Can set in when climbers do not have enough warm, protective clothing, healthy food or water. It is caused by a rapid loss of body heat. A person's body temperature falls below normal, causing muscle and brain functions to become impaired.
Symptoms	Headache, loss of appetite, dizziness, drowsiness, vomiting, unable to sleep, short breaths, tiredness. May lead to death.	Extreme tiredness, numbness, shivering, slurred speech, odd behaviour, stumbling, dizzy spells and muscle cramps.
Treatments	Stop climbing and rest for a day or so at a lower altitude until symptoms stop.	Call a doctor. Move inside, replace wet clothing and drink warm fluids.
Prevention	Climb 500 metres maximum per day, resting every third day.	Keep warm with layered clothing, and avoid long-term exposure to the cold.

"The death zone" is the term used by mountain climbers to describe altitudes higher than 8,000 metres. At this level, there is barely enough oxygen for people to survive. Even when using bottled oxygen, climbers can experience ill health.

Frostbite	Dehydration
When body tissue under the skin becomes frozen and stops oxygen from getting to that part of the body. Frostbite normally affects the hands, feet, ears, nose and cheeks.	When the body loses a lot of fluid through sweating, vomiting and fever, or by not drinking enough liquids. This prevents vital organs such as the heart, kidneys and brain from functioning properly.
Wax-like skin with a white, greyish-yellow, or blue colour. The affected parts will be numb with blisters. Swelling, itching, burning and deep pain occurs as the area is warmed again.	Weakness and thirst may lead to drowsiness, fainting or coma.
Place affected parts in warm water or blankets, but do not rub the skin.	Drink a rehydration liquid, such as a sports drink, for severe fluid loss.
Wear scarves, earmuffs, hats, balaclavas, mittens or gloves, two pairs of wool socks and ankle boots.	Drink 3–5 litres of water a day.

This situation, along with the threat of avalanches, crevasses, fierce winds and freezing temperatures, helps explain why around 290 people have died trying to climb Mount Everest. To date, around 200 corpses remain there.

Chapter 7

Rescues in wild places

What's your opinion?

People who enjoy adventures in remote, wild places often experience a great sense of personal freedom and achievement. Many people, however, believe such thrill seekers take pointless risks, when there are lots of other ways to have fun. The costs involved in major rescue operations or long-term illnesses help support this view.

I love being outdoors. When I reach the mountain's **summit**, there are breathtaking views of nature. Training for a climb makes me feel healthy and strong.

When I dive into the deep ocean, I get a huge rush of adrenaline. There are risks, but I train hard and feel well prepared for any difficulties I might encounter. Besides, life has many other dangers.

When I go caving, I know I am taking great risks. I try to be careful. If I get into trouble I don't expect other people to risk their lives to save me.

Some rescue operations cost millions of dollars. The money used on these rescues would be better spent on charities that benefit larger numbers of people.

I think that these adventurers should be more aware of the dangers in these places, and how others put their lives at risk to save them when things go wrong.

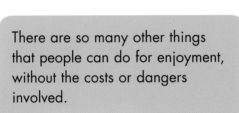

There are so many other things that people can do for enjoyment, without the costs or dangers involved.

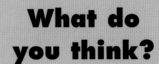

What do you think?

10 January 1997

Adventurer rescued after five days at sea

A British yachtsman has been rescued by emergency services in the Southern Ocean. Tony Bullimore was feared drowned after his yacht overturned five days ago, but was found in the boat's upturned hull. He had been in a race around the world.

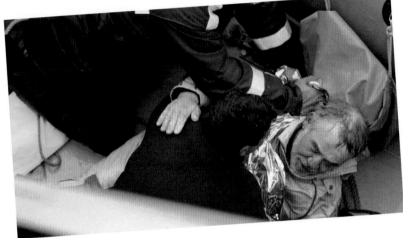

Upon being rescued, Mr Bullimore was "absolutely ecstatic". He had a small amount of chocolate and water to keep him going, and had been wearing a survival suit to protect him from the extreme cold.

It is believed Mr Bullimore probably had only enough air to last six days in the small area where he was trapped. "He is very lucky to be alive," a rescue coordinator said. Now in the hospital, Mr Bullimore is recovering from mild **hypothermia** and **dehydration**. He is about to receive decompression treatment.

"He is very lucky to be alive"

Mr Bullimore's wife, who is flying out to be with her husband, said, "He is a true survivor." Even so, questions are now being raised over the cost of such a large rescue procedure, and the major risk of sailing solo in the ocean.

Glossary

air pressure the force of air on objects, mainly referring to air in a small space like a tyre or oxygen tank

altitude the height measured from sea level, usually for high places like mountains

belaying holding the rope taut to stop one's rock climbing partner from falling

blizzard an extreme snowstorm that can last for days

buoyant able to float

chambers small, compartment-like rooms

crevasses deep cracks formed on a glacier or in the earth's surface

dehydration when the body loses a lot of water

dysentery a disease caused by an infection that results in severe diarrhoea

expedition a journey made by an organised group to reach an exact destination

fatigue extreme tiredness of the mind or body from hard work

frostbite damage caused to body tissue by freezing

fungus a type of living thing

hypothermia an illness marked by a very low body temperature, caused by cold and wet conditions

itinerary a travel plan that includes a route and a schedule

moonscapes areas thought to look like the landscape of the moon

nylon an artificial fabric that is light but strong

oxygen an important gas in the air that is vital for living things to survive

paralysed unable to move or feel anything in a certain part of the body

Sherpa member of a Tibetan tribe living near Mount Everest; some Sherpas travel with the climbers because of their knowledge of the mountain

stagnant water still water where bacteria breed because rain doesn't flush them out

summit the top of a mountain

symptoms the signs that point to a certain illness

trek a slow, difficult journey

trekking to travel slowly

Index